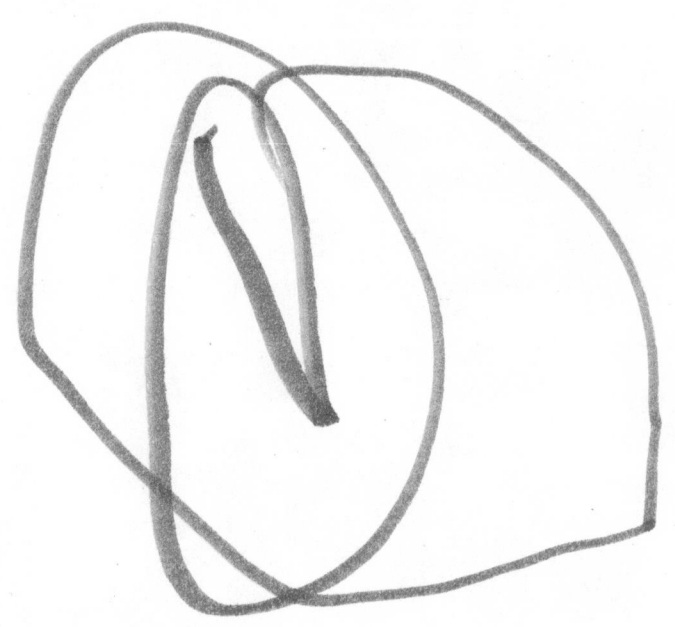

Eyes on the Sky

The Moon

by Don Nardo

KIDHAVEN PRESS™

THOMSON

GALE

San Diego • Detroit • New York • San Francisco • Cleveland
New Haven, Conn. • Waterville, Maine • London • Munich

THOMSON
GALE

Cover Photo and Title Page photo: © Larry Landolfi/Photo Researchers (main);
  © Gazelle Technologies
© Chris Butler/Science Source/Photo Researchers, 30
© Corel Corporation, 17, 33
© Dr. F. Espenak/Photo Researchers, Inc., 21
Grace Fryar, 16, 19
© Mark Garlick/Science Source/Photo Researchers, 7, 8, 12, 26, 34
© Gazelle Technologies, 5, 24, 36
© Victor Habbick Visions/Photo Researchers, 28
© Cindy Kassab/CORBIS, 22
© Larry Landolfi/Photo Researchers, 15
© NASA/Roger Ressmeyer/CORBIS, 27
© Pat O'Hara/CORBIS, 38
© Roger Ressmeyer/CORBIS, 10
© Kevin Schafer/CORBIS, 40

LIBRARY OF CONGRESS CATALOGING-IN-PUBLICATION DATA

Nardo, Don, 1947–
  The moon / by Don Nardo.
   v. cm.—(Eyes on the sky)
Includes bibliographical references and index.
Summary: Discusses the birth of the moon, moon exploration, its physical
qualities, and what it would be like without a moon.
  ISBN 0-7377-1291-0 (hardback : alk. paper)
1. Moon—Juvenile literature. [1. Moon.} I. Title. II. Series.
  QB582 .N37   2003
  523.3—dc21

2001003811

Table of Contents

1

The Moon's Violent Birth

Except for the sun, the moon is the most prominent and familiar object in the sky. Each month the moon travels across the sky, its phases changing slowly but steadily from crescent to full and then back again. Human beings have observed these phases for thousands of years. In ancient times humans saw the phases, along with the moon itself, as somehow supernatural; cultures around the world developed various moon-related religious and folk beliefs. Many viewed it as a god or other powerful being. In this guise it determined or oversaw fate, the passage of time, plant growth, or rainfall. The early Romans, for instance, held that the moon was a goddess named Luna. This is the origin of the word *lunar*, still used to describe various aspects of the moon.

Modern science has shown that the moon is actually Earth's only natural satellite. Its phases derive from the changing way the sun illuminates it as it **orbits** Earth. The moon is also our nearest neighbor in space. And as such, it has come to be seen as the first stepping-stone in space exploration. This is why the United States

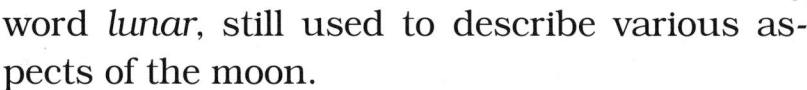

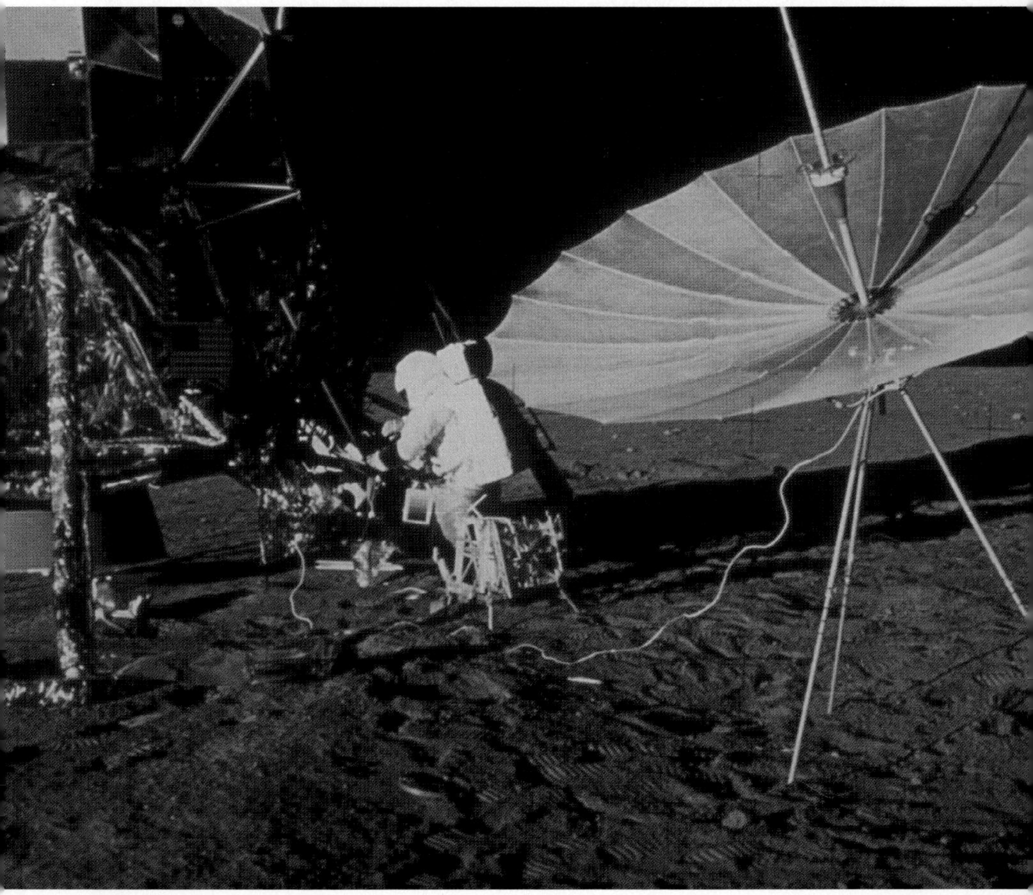

An astronaut gathers soil samples from the lunar surface in 1969.

landed the first humans on the lunar surface in 1969. Astronauts studied the moon up close. They brought back samples of lunar rocks and dust which were analyzed, greatly expanding knowledge about the moon. In particular, scientists found important clues to solving the mystery of the moon's origins.

The Capture Theory

Before astronauts went to the moon, astronomers had three main theories for how the moon formed. The first is the **capture theory**. It proposes that the moon did not form near Earth. Instead, the moon was originally a small **planet** moving in an independent orbit around the sun.

In that case, the moon formed the same way Earth and other planets did. A vast cloud of gas and dust surrounded the infant sun. In time, some of the particles of gas and dust began to stick to one another, creating larger pieces. In this process, called **accretion**, the pieces steadily formed larger and larger clumps. Astronomers call these clumps—which measured between a few thousand feet and a few miles—**planetesimals**. Large planetesimals had enough **gravity** to begin pulling in even more matter; so these quickly grew into massive objects. And the biggest of these objects became the planets, including the moon.

The gravity of a planet pulls in planetesimals and other space debris.

According to the capture theory, the moon eventually strayed too close to Earth. The strong gravity of Earth yanked the moon from its orbit and captured it. Ever since that time the moon has been Earth's satellite. This theory predicts that, because the moon formed far from Earth, the composition of the two bodies would be noticeably different.

Lunar Origins Closer to Home

The second theory proposes that the moon formed right beside Earth. According to this view, the two bodies emerged out of the same section of the original cloud of gas and dust. In a way, they were twins; so this idea is called the **twin formation theory**. It holds that the early Earth and moon drew in similar elements in similar concentrations; so it stands to reason that their compositions will be similar.

As they formed, Earth and the moon were bombarded by meteors, asteroids, and comets.

Finally, the so-called **fission theory** suggests that the moon was once actually a part of Earth. The term *fission* means to split into parts. Supposedly, the early Earth **rotated**, or spun, on its **axis**, faster and faster. Eventually this created a large bulge. And the bulge broke away and became the moon. If this theory is correct, the composition of the two bodies will be not just similar, but exactly the same.

Surprises from the Lunar Rocks

The actual composition of the moon is a key factor, therefore, in deciding which theory for lunar origins is correct. So not surprisingly, scientists were excited as they prepared to examine the moon rocks brought back by the astronauts. For the first time in history, researchers would be able to analyze in a lab pieces of the moon. And the moon's composition would be revealed at last. The scientists fully expected to find evidence confirming one of the three prevailing theories—capture, twin formation, or fission.

To their surprise, however, these researchers found that the evidence did not support any of the theories. The composition of the moon rocks was not completely identical to that of Earth. Nor was it completely different.

A scientist examines a small slice of moon rock under a microscope.

On the one hand, scientists found that the moon contains certain concentrations of oxygen and other elements exactly like those on Earth. This rules out the capture theory; if it was correct, these concentrations would not be identical. On the other hand, concentrations of some other elements are different on the moon than on Earth. This calls the fission theory into serious question. If it was correct, concentrations of all the elements should be the same in both bodies. The moon also contains extremely little iron, whereas Earth has a great deal of iron. If the twin formation theory was correct, the two bodies would have similar amounts of iron.

A Disastrous Impact

Thus, the evidence from the moon rocks pointed scientists toward a new theory of lunar formation. In 1975 an important paper appeared in the scientific journal *Icarus*. The authors were William K. Hartmann and Donald R. Davis of the Planetary Science Institute in Tucson, Arizona. They proposed that the moon originated when a large cosmic object crashed into the infant Earth. The object was perhaps the size of the planet Mars (which has about half the diameter and one-tenth the **mass** of Earth). So it was probably a young planet that passed too close to Earth.

The impact of the two bodies was disastrous. Large sections of both shattered and melted. And the smaller object was absorbed, its iron core merging with Earth's own iron core. Meanwhile, millions of cubic miles of material from the crusts of the two bodies was thrown into space. Some of this material escaped Earth's gravity and floated away into space. But most remained in orbit. Over time, it cooled and its own gravity made it contract into a **sphere**, or ball. Today we called that ball the moon.

Illustrated here are the three stages of the impact theory: the impact; material thrown into orbit; and Earth with its new companion, the moon.

This **impact theory** neatly explains a wide range of evidence and observations. First, it accounts for the composition of the moon rocks. They contain little iron because the moon formed mainly from material in Earth's crust; most of the iron on Earth exists in its core, and the crust contains only small amounts of iron. Also, those moon substances identical to the ones on Earth came from Earth. And the lunar substances having a different composition than those on Earth came from the impacting body.

Earth's Axis

The impact theory also explains an important fact about Earth's axis, the imaginary pole around which it spins. The axes of most other planets stand upright; but Earth's is tipped at an angle. (This causes the amount of sunlight reaching various parts of the planet to vary somewhat during the course of a year; and the result is changes of season in many parts of the globe.) The impact of the object that formed the moon likely knocked Earth partway over.

These theories about the moon's origin have one thing in common. Namely, they all picture it as a catastrophic event. When astronauts visited the moon, they found it a silent and peaceful place. Only by examining the evidence hidden in its rocks can one tell that it was born out of unimaginable violence.

2
A Silent and Desolate World

Seen both with the naked eye and through telescopes, the moon looks gray, deserted, and lifeless. And in fact, it is. Unlike Earth, the moon has no air, water, or life. One of the first astronauts to set foot on the moon called it a place of magnificent desolation, or barrenness.

Not only is the moon barren, but its lack of an atmosphere also makes it a world of stark extremes. Earth's atmosphere creates wind and weather. It also keeps temperatures moderate, so it does not become too hot or too cold in most parts of the globe and makes the sky look blue in the daytime. In addition, the air carries sound, so that people and animals can hear.

By contrast, the moon's surface is either very hot or very cold. On the sunlit side, temperatures can reach as high as 265°F at midday. That is 53° hotter than the boiling point of water. (Of course, the moon has no water to boil!) Meanwhile, on the dark side the temperature plummets to as low as –170°F. No trace of wind sweeps the moon's surface; no sound can be heard; and the sky is always black, even in the daytime.

Footprints in the Dust

The moon lacks more than an atmosphere and the life-supporting properties of air. Earth's satellite is as dead on the inside as it is on the outside. The moon's rocky core generates almost no heat. So no volcanoes erupt, spread lava, and thereby change the little world's surface features.

This view of the moon in its crescent phase shows it to be a gray, barren world.

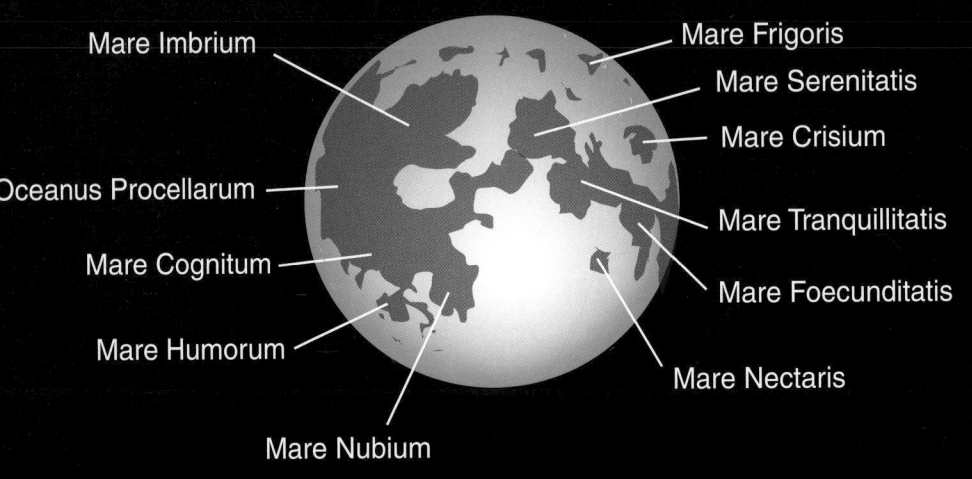

Moon's Maria

Mare Imbrium

Mare Frigoris

Mare Serenitatis

Mare Crisium

Oceanus Procellarum

Mare Tranquillitatis

Mare Cognitum

Mare Foecunditatis

Mare Humorum

Mare Nectaris

Mare Nubium

Among the most prominent features of the moon are large, flat, dark areas, some of them hundreds of miles wide. They are known as **maria** (pronounced MAR-ee-a). The term is Latin for seas; the maria are visible to the naked eye from Earth and from far away they do look a bit like large bodies of water. In reality, though, they are as dry and barren as the rest of the moon's surface. Early astronomers gave the maria poetic names, such as the Sea of Serenity and the Sea of Tranquility.

Surrounding the flat maria are the lunar highlands. These are rugged plateaus covered with craters of all sizes. The craters range from an inch or less across to as much as 150 miles

(240 kilometers) in diameter. Many of the craters, which number in the millions, are visible through ordinary binoculars.

Most of these surface features have undergone little change since the era just after the moon formed. Because the moon has no atmosphere and no volcanic activity, there is nothing that will erode, or wear down, the maria, craters, and other surface features. So they stay the same year after year. In fact, the footprints the astronauts left in the lunar dust will probably still be there 1 or 2 million years from now.

This footprint left by an astronaut in the lunar dust will likely remain there for millions of years.

A Double Planet

It is not surprising that many lunar surface features are readily visible to the eye or through binoculars or small telescopes. First, the moon is large. It is 2,140 miles (3,476 km) across, about a quarter the diameter of Earth; and the moon's mass equals about $1/81$ that of Earth's. That is unusually large for a satellite when compared to its parent planet. And accordingly, the Earth-moon system is sometimes referred to as a double planet. (Most satellites are less than $1/500$ the size of the planets they orbit; only Pluto's moon, Charon, is larger than Earth's moon in relation to its parent.)

The moon is also quite close to Earth as compared to other heavenly bodies. The average distance between the moon and Earth is 250,000 miles (380,000 km), about thirty-one times Earth's diameter. At that distance, it takes the moon about 27.3 days to orbit Earth once.

The moon's unusual size and closeness to Earth cause a strange phenomenon in the Earth-moon system. Over time, the pull of their mutual gravities slows the rate at which each rotates, or spins, on its axis. The moon still rotates. But its period of rotation exactly equals its period of revolution around Earth. For that reason the smaller body eternally keeps the same

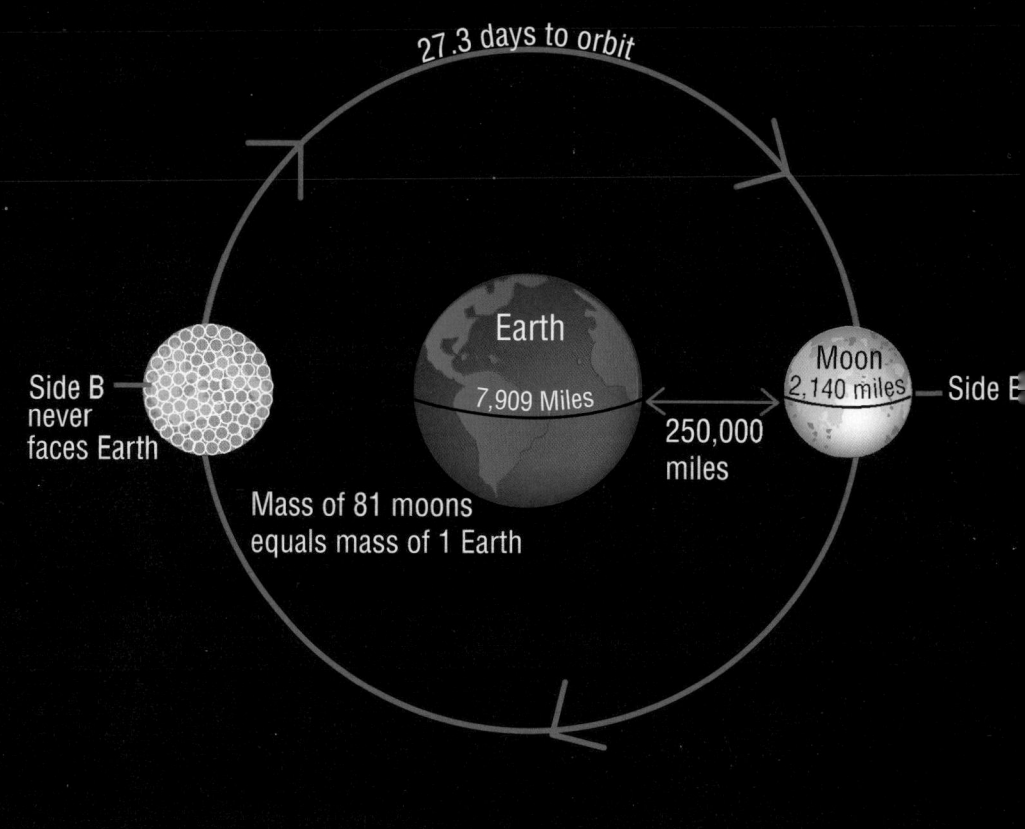

27.3 days to orbit

Earth

7,909 Miles

Side B never faces Earth

Moon
2,140 miles — Side E

250,000 miles

Mass of 81 moons equals mass of 1 Earth

side facing its parent. In fact, humanity did not catch its first glimpse of the far side of the moon until 1959. In that year the Russian spacecraft *Luna 3* flew around and photographed it, revealing surface features like those on the more familiar side.

At the same time, the relentless pull of lunar gravity is causing Earth's rotation to slow. The length of a day on Earth is growing longer by a very tiny amount each century. Many millions of years from now, Earth and the moon will be locked in a strange embrace. A day on Earth will last fifty times longer than it does today.

Meanwhile, the moon will no longer rotate; and it will move around Earth in the same period—fifty days. In this odd situation, a day and month will be the same length. Also, to a person living on the side of Earth facing the moon, that object will forever remain fixed in the same spot in the sky. And a person living on the other side of Earth will never see the moon at all.

Eclipses and the Tides

Today, the way in which the moon moves around Earth does more than determine the length of a month. It also causes some truly spectacular cosmic shows—eclipses. From time to time, the moon passes directly between the sun and Earth. By coincidence, the moon's disk is about the same width as the sun's as seen from Earth. So the moon momentarily covers the sun's face, turning day into night. This is called a solar eclipse.

The moon also plays a prominent role in lunar eclipses. These occur when the moon passes into the shadow that Earth casts as the sun shines on it. For an hour or more, the moon's disk turns a deep red, almost the color of blood. This eerie, beautiful sight never fails

An eclipse of the sun as seen from the ancient ruins of Stonehenge in England.

to impress people, especially those viewing it for the first time.

Another lunar effect on Earth—tides—are caused by lunar gravity. As our satellite moves along in its orbit, its gravity pulls on Earth's oceans. And the water bulges slightly on both the side facing the moon and the side facing away from it. As Earth rotates, the tidal bulges move across its surface; and when they reach the edges of the land masses, the water crawls up the shores in the form of high tides. Because there are two tidal bulges, high tide occurs twice

The full moon can be seen above some ocean waves, a reminder that the moon's gravity causes the tides.

a day. (The sun's gravity also contributes to the tides; but because it is so far away, its tidal force on Earth is only about a third of the moon's.) The tides are one way that the stark and lifeless moon directly affects the billions of life forms on its parent world.

3
Formation of Craters and Maria

The sight of the moon's surface through a small telescope is stunning and compelling, no matter how many times one sees it. The lunar highlands are choked with craters of all sizes and jagged, rocky peaks. In stark contrast, the maria are darker and smoother; far fewer craters litter their surfaces than those of the rugged highlands. Looking at these features, one cannot help but sense that all were created by enormously violent events.

For a long time astronomers wondered about the nature of these violent events. And they came to the conclusion that the moon's surface features were shaped mainly by volcanism. This process is a familiar one on Earth. The interior of the planet is very hot. At

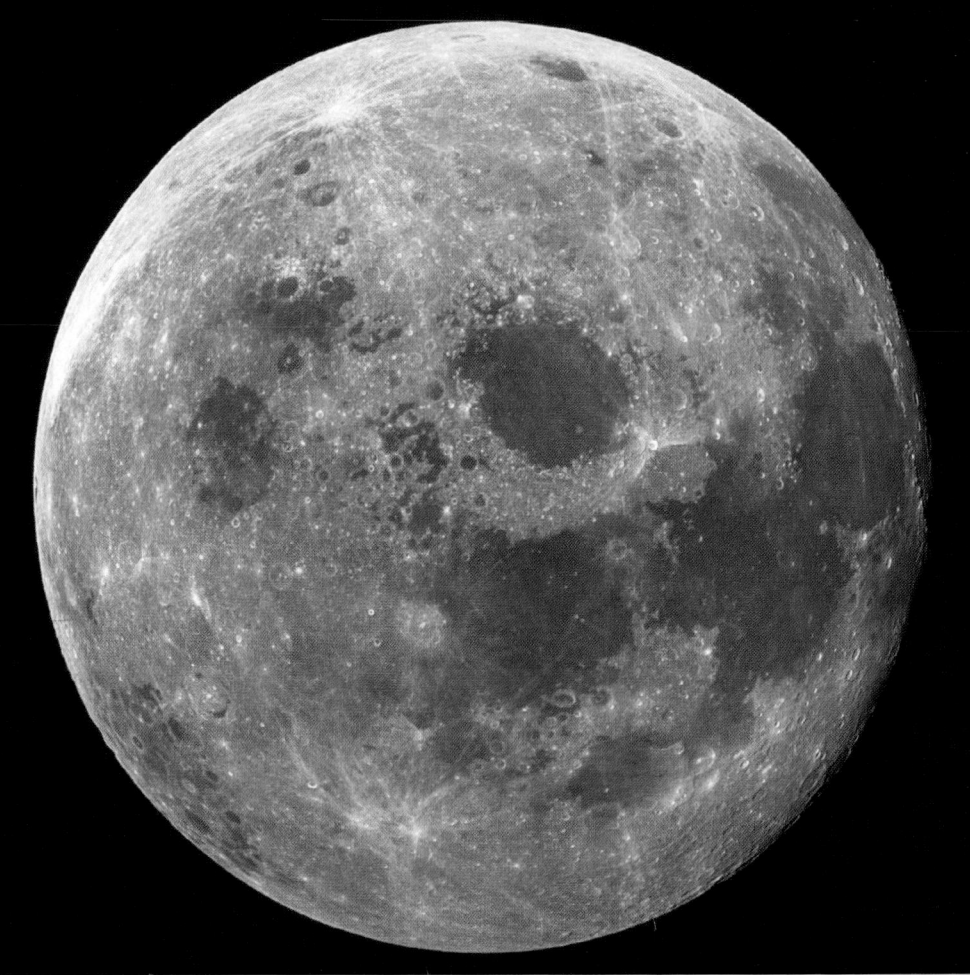

Craters and maria are visible over the moon's surface.

a certain depth the heat is intense enough to melt solid rock. And at times the melted rock, called magma, makes its way to the surface and bursts forth in a volcanic eruption. (When the magma reaches the surface, it is called lava.)

This same process, scientists suggest, had once occurred all over the moon. According to this view, most of the craters visible today are the remnants of ancient volcanoes. And the flat, smoother maria are ancient lava flows.

volcanic theory of the origins of the surface features is now known to be wrong and partly right. It is wrong re- g the lunar craters. In the 1970s the as- tr ts who landed on the moon studied these craters close-up; and other researchers studied similar craters on Earth. The studies showed that the craters formed not in volcanic eruptions but from the impacts caused by colli- sions with cosmic objects. On the other hand, the same studies showed that the maria were indeed created by volcanism, although the moon is no longer volcanically active.

Cosmic Disasters

When discussing the subject of cosmic impacts on the moon and Earth, one question always comes up: Why did the moon undergo more bombardment than Earth? The moon is heavily cratered, while very few impact craters exist on Earth. This would seem to make little sense. After all, Earth is much more massive and has considerably stronger gravity than the moon. So Earth should have pulled in more asteroids, comets, and other space debris than the moon did; and Earth's surface should have more craters.

In reality, Earth *did* pull in more space de- bris than the moon did. And the result was more crater formation over time. In fact, giant

The dinosaurs met their doom when a cosmic object collided with Earth.

impacts have caused huge disasters on Earth in the past. For example, most scientists believe that the impact of an asteroid or comet about 65 million years ago wiped out the dinosaurs.

Like other such impacts, the one that killed the dinosaurs left a large crater. However, Earth has an atmosphere, which produces weather effects such as rain and wind. Also, the planet remains volcanically active. The effects of rain, wind, waves, and flowing lava slowly but surely wear down, fill in, and erase most impact craters. The big crater created 65 million years ago now lies buried beneath the seabed off the eastern coast of Mexico.

Like Millions of Nuclear Bombs

Obviously the moon has no seas and weather to hide its craters. So the evidence of the impacts that formed them remains clearly visible. Lunar craters have rim walls—steep piles of rock—lining their circular edges. These walls are sometimes hundreds or even thousands of feet high. And cracks and long trails of rocky debris stretch outward for miles in all directions from the larger craters.

The rim walls of these craters formed when lunar material splashed outward during impacts.

The cosmic impacts that blasted and displaced these billions of tons of rock were extremely violent events. Typically, an impacting object, or **impactor**, is moving very fast as it approaches the surface. Speeds of 12 miles (20 km) per second or more are fairly normal for cosmic bodies. In human terms, though, such speeds are almost beyond comprehension.

The impactor's great speed combines with its mass to create a huge amount of stored-up energy. It remains potential and harmless energy only as long as the object moves undis-

A large object smashes into the moon, creating a new crater.

turbed through space. But when it strikes the moon's surface, the stored-up energy is suddenly released. The larger the impactor's mass and speed, the larger is the energy released. An object 6 miles (10 km) in diameter traveling at 20 miles per second would create an explosion millions of times greater than that of a nuclear bomb.

When such an impactor strikes the moon's surface, this enormous explosion vaporizes most of the object. Meanwhile, some of the lunar material at ground zero melts. Most, however, is shattered and pushed outward in all directions. The impact is so violent that the mass of this material is about ten thousand times greater than that of the impactor itself. Eventually, the dislodged lunar material slows down and piles up, forming the rim wall of the crater.

Creation of the Lunar Maria

Most of the major impacts that created lunar craters occurred shortly after the moon formed. By contrast, volcanism created the maria close to a billion years later. To understand why, consider the moon's development in its first billion years. First, material blasted off Earth by a collision with a planet-sized object slowly contracted to form the moon. At first, the lunar surface was molten, or liquid. But as it cooled, a hard outer crust formed.

For several million years, cosmic debris rained down on the infant moon, cratering this crust. Eventually, the rate of bombardment decreased. But a few extremely large objects struck, leaving behind enormous craterlike basins. These impacts also created cracks that stretched downward into the moon's interior. That interior was still molten and very hot. So magma steadily oozed up through the cracks and filled the basins, creating the maria.

Magma oozes through a giant lunar crack about 3 billion years ago.

End of Volcanism

The maria formed between 3.5 and 4 billion years ago. By this time, cosmic impacts had become fairly rare; to this day, therefore, relatively few craters mar the smooth surfaces of the maria. Over time, the moon continued to cool and its interior largely solidified. So volcanism ceased. In this way, a cosmic body that endured millions of years of violence and upheaval became the dead, unchanging orb that rules Earth's night sky.

4
What If There Were No Moon?

Most people take the moon—and the ways in which it affects Earth—for granted. Without fail, our satellite spins around its parent once each month. So people can count on seeing the moon go through its cycle of phases month after month, year after year, century after century. They can predict eclipses far into the future; this allows people to enjoy and study these cosmic shows at their leisure. The daily march of the tides is also taken for granted. Billions of sea animals and birds hunt, mate, and nest in sync with the rising and falling coastal waters. And humans plan activities—ranging from sailing to fishing to sunbathing—around the tides.

These are among the more obvious ways the moon affects Earth and its living things. Yet there are many less obvious ways. In fact, the moon's presence has been crucial in the **evolution**, or ongoing change, of the planet. The moon has helped to shape Earth's geography and atmosphere. And the development of life on Earth has been profoundly influenced by the moon. Indeed, consider how different Earth and its life forms would be if the moon had never formed.

Lower Tides and Shorter Days

First, the moon would not exist today had not a planet-sized object struck Earth about 4.5 billion years ago. That huge impactor gouged out

Activities such as sailing are planned around the tides which are caused by the moon.

a massive basin in Earth's crust. It also caused large amounts of magma to burst forth from below. Enormous lava flows then reshaped much of Earth's surface. These were major factors in determining the sizes and shapes of the ocean basins and continents. Thus, if the ancient impactor had not struck, Earth's geography would be very different today.

Earth's tides would also be different if the ancient impactor had not caused the moon to form. Even without the moon, Earth would have tides. But these would be caused solely by the sun. So they would be only one-third as high as the ones on Earth today.

The infant moon looms large in the sky above the early Earth.

In the past 4.5 billion years, these sun-generated tides have caused the seas to scrape along the bottoms of the ocean basins. Over time, this has slowed Earth's rotation and the days have become longer. But the moon's gravity has played a much larger role than the sun's in slowing the planet's spin. Together, the moon and sun have caused the day to lengthen from six to twenty-four hours. If there were no moon, by contrast, Earth's rotation would have slowed much less. A day would presently be just eight hours long. So the sun would race across the daytime sky in only three to five hours; and a year would consist of 1,095 eight-hour days.

A Windswept Planet

Earth's rate of rotation also affects its atmosphere, including the winds. The faster a planet with an atmosphere spins, the faster and stronger its winds. With no moon and an eight-hour day, Earth's winds would be very strong indeed. They would travel mainly from east to west; and they would constantly blow at sixty, seventy, or more miles per hour. Such winds would make ocean waves higher and more violent, causing more beach erosion. Also, hurricanes would be much larger and stronger. And wind and rain would wear down mountains much faster; the highest peaks on the globe

A large hurricane in midocean. Without the moon, such storms would be even larger.

would be a good deal lower than those on Earth today.

The atmosphere's composition would also be very different if the moon did not exist. Today, Earth's air is about 78 percent nitrogen and 21 percent oxygen (with smaller amounts of other gases). But the atmosphere was originally quite different. It was made up mainly of carbon dioxide, nitrogen, and water vapor. And the air was about 115 times thicker than it is now. When the ancient impactor struck Earth, it ripped away part of the atmosphere, causing it to thin. Eventually, the first tiny plants appeared in the seas. They took in carbon dioxide as food and gave off oxygen as a waste material; so levels of oxygen in the air slowly increased.

In contrast, if the ancient impactor had never struck Earth and formed the moon, carbon dioxide levels would have remained high. This would have made the planet much hotter. And primitive ocean life would have taken longer to evolve. In addition, the buildup of oxygen in the air would have taken hundreds of millions of years longer. And many of the plants and animals that developed would have been different.

Life Emerges on the Moonless Earth

The absence of the moon would have affected the evolution of life in other ways as well. For example, scientists believe that the chemical building blocks of life floated in the primitive seas. The crucial areas were the shallow waters near the coasts. The chemicals filtered into calm pools created by the tides; repeatedly warmed by the sun and struck by lightning, these substances came together to form the microscopic building blocks of living cells. Today, Earth's coastal margins remain rich with life. There, a great diversity of plants, shellfish, insects, birds, and other living things thrive.

Without the moon, however, the much weaker tides would create fewer and smaller tidal pools. So primitive life forms would emerge less often; and they would be more widely spaced. Also, the higher winds and more violent waves would disrupt the delicate life-building process. If life developed at all, it would take much longer for it to gain a strong foothold.

Assuming that life did manage to gain a foothold on the moonless Earth, plants and animals would remain in the seas for a long time.

Without the moon, many forms of ocean life that exist today would never have developed.

But eventually they would emerge onto the land. And they would face an extremely hostile environment. The constant high winds would bend and uproot the taller plants; so there would be no tall trees for a long time, if ever. Instead, plants would grow close to the ground, develop wide, heavy stems, and anchor themselves with deep roots.

Animals would need to adapt to the punishing winds, too. They would develop wide bodies with short legs; that would keep them low to the ground and less likely to be blown over. Many would also have long claws to dig into ground for extra stability. And most would grow thick skins or shells; these would reduce the chance of injury from airborne sand and rocks. In addition, wind disperses sound, making it harder to hear; so such animals would develop a very keen sense of hearing. This ability would aid them at night, too. With no moon, there would be no moonlight to hunt by. So they would need to find prey by zeroing in on the sounds of their movements.

Products of a Different Evolution

Eventually, after several billion years, intelligent life might emerge on the moonless Earth. But these beings would be the product of a very different course of evolution than the one that gave rise to human beings. Such beings would surely look different. Perhaps they would have squat bodies with thick legs and large ears. Similarly, they would develop different languages, customs, and social values.

The beings on the moonless Earth would also view the heavens differently. Lacking the moon, they would recognize neither months

This alligator can hunt at night without seeing its prey. Animals on a moonless Earth would need the same ability.

nor a lunar calendar. They would see no eclipses. And having no natural satellite, they would lack a convenient stepping-stone to the stars. The planets Venus and Mars would be their nearest cosmic neighbors. These planets lie hundreds of times farther from Earth than the moon does. So the beings would likely be less inclined to launch astronauts into space.

These are only some of the ways that Earth would be different if the moon had never formed. Clearly then, the moon has shaped Earth in countless important ways. And the human race owes much of its present existence to our planet's lifeless but dependable companion.

Glossary

accretion: A process in which small pieces of a substance stick together to form larger pieces.

axis: An imaginary pole in the center of a planet or other cosmic body around which that object spins.

capture theory: The idea that the moon formed far from Earth, and Earth's larger gravity captured the smaller body.

evolution: Ongoing change over the course of time.

fission theory: The idea that the moon formed when a bulge formed in and broke away from the rapidly spinning young Earth.

gravity: A force exerted by an object that attracts other objects. The pull of Earth's gravity keeps rocks, people, and houses from floating away into space. It also holds the moon in its orbit around Earth.

impactor: An object that crashes into another object, creating a measurable impact.

impact theory: The idea that the moon formed from material blasted off the young Earth's surface by the impact of Earth with another early planet.

maria: Large, flat, smooth areas on the moon. Scientists believe that the maria formed when lava filled large craterlike basins.

mass: The total amount of matter contained in an object.

orbit: To move around something; or the path taken by a planet or other heavenly body around the sun, or a moon around a planet.

planet: A large, spherical object that orbits a star independently and shines by reflected, rather than its own, light.

planetesimals: Small objects that orbited the early sun and combined to form the planets.

rotate: To spin around a central axis.

sphere: A round shape, like a ball.

twin formation theory: The idea that the moon originated beside Earth and that both objects formed from the same cloud of gas and dust.

For Further Exploration

Isaac Asimov, *What Is an Eclipse?* Milwaukee: Gareth Stevens, 1991. One of the greatest science explainers of the twentieth century tells about the moon's involvement in solar and lunar eclipses.

Pam Beasant, *1000 Facts About Space.* New York: Kingfisher Books, 1992. An informative collection of basic facts about the stars, planets, asteroids, and other heavenly bodies.

Neil F. Comins, *What If the Moon Didn't Exist? Voyages to Earths That Might Have Been.* New York: HarperCollins, 1993. An astronomer explores what Earth would be like if the moon had never formed. The text is challenging for young readers but worth the effort.

Robert Gardner, *Science Project Ideas About the Moon.* Berkeley Heights, NJ: Enslow, 1997. An excellent collection of ideas for student projects about the moon.

Nigel Henbest, *DK Space Encyclopedia.* London: Dorling Kindersley, 1999. This beautifully mounted and critically acclaimed book is the best general source available for grade-school readers about the wonders of space.

Maria B. Jacobs and Nancy Ellwood, *Why Do the Oceans Have Tides?* New York: Rosen Publishing Group, 1999. Explains the workings of one of the major ways the moon affects Earth.

Robin Kerrod, *The Children's Space Atlas: A Voyage of Discovery for Young Astronauts.* Brookfield, CT: Millbrook Press, 1992. A well-written, informative explanation of the stars, planets, comets, asteroids, and other objects making up the universe.

Don Nardo, *The Solar System.* San Diego: KidHaven Press, 2002. A fact-filled overview of the many and diverse cosmic bodies making up the sun's family.

Carole Stott, *DK Discoveries: Moon Landing.* London: Dorling Kindersley, 1999. Like this publisher's other books for young people, this one about the moon is well written, informative, and lavishly illustrated. Highly recommended.

Anastasia Suen, *Man on the Moon*. New York: Viking Children's Books, 1997. Written for very young, basic readers, this overview of facts about the moon is handsomely illustrated.

Index

OUR GREAT STATES

WHAT'S GREAT ABOUT
MASSACHUSETTS?

✳ Amanda Lanser

⌊ LERNER PUBLICATIONS COMPANY ✳ MINNEAPOLIS

CONTENTS

MASSACHUSETTS WELCOMES YOU! ✳ 4

Content Consultant: Samuel Redman, Assistant Professor, Department of History and Center for Heritage and Society, University of Massachusetts Amherst

Lerner Publications Company
A division of Lerner Publishing Group, Inc.
241 First Avenue North
Minneapolis, MN 55401 USA

For reading levels and more information, look up this title at www.lernerbooks.com.

Main body text set in ITC Franklin Gothic Std Book Condensed 12/15.
Typeface provided by Adobe Systems.

Library of Congress Cataloging-in-Publication Data

Lanser, Amanda.
    What's great about Massachusetts? / by Amanda Lanser.
        pages   cm. — (Our great states)
    Includes index.
    ISBN 978-1-4677-3331-1 (lib. bdg. : alk. paper)
    ISBN 978-1-4677-4710-3 (eBook)
    1. Massachusetts—Juvenile literature.
    I. Title.
    F64.3.L36 2014
    974.4—dc23   2013042392

Manufactured in the United States of America

1 – PC – 7/15/14

MASSACHUSETTS Welcomes You!

That's the warm greeting you'll see as you enter the Bay State. You may spot the state's official flower, the mayflower, on the welcome sign. You'll see the state's official bird, the black-capped chickadee, too. Massachusetts has something for everyone. Grab your towel and sunscreen. Head to the beaches on the Cape Cod National Seashore. Don't forget to try some of the freshest seafood anywhere. Go for a drive on the Mohawk Trail. Take in the beauty of the Berkshire Hills. Massachusetts's culture and history are older than the United States itself. That makes towns like Lexington and Concord exciting places for history fans. Do you like city life? You'll fall in love with hip and historic Boston. Read on to learn more about the top ten things Massachusetts has to offer.

NEW YORK

VERMONT

NEW HAMPSHIRE

ATLANTIC OCEAN

▲ Mount Williams
▲ Mount Greylock

Connecticut River

Wachusett Mountain ▲

Merrimack River

Lowell

Cape Ann

BERKSHIRE HILLS

● Lenox

East Mountain ▲

Amherst ●

Nashua River

Concord ●

Lexington ●

Lynn ●

Mystic River

Cambridge ●

Boston ✦

Concord River

Boston Harbor

Massachusetts Bay

N

● Worcester

Quincy ●

Springfield ●

Charles River

Brockton ●

CONNECTICUT

RHODE ISLAND

Taunton River

Plymouth ●

Cape Cod National Seashore

Cape Cod

Cape Cod Bay

Fall River ●

Miles
0   10   20
0   10   20   30
Kilometers

New Bedford ●

Martha's Vineyard

Nantucket Island

Explore Massachusetts's major cities and all the places in between! Just turn the page to find out all about THE BAY STATE. >

CAPE COD NATIONAL SEASHORE

> Ready to dig your toes into the sand? Do you want to feel the salt on your skin? Plan a trip to Cape Cod National Seashore! A cape is a point of land that extends out into a body of water. In this case, the body of water is the Atlantic Ocean. Cape Cod is at the easternmost tip of Massachusetts. This 40-mile (64 kilometer) coastline includes beaches, ponds, and woods.

Pedal to the beach on the Cape Cod Rail Trail. It starts in central Cape Cod. You can bike all the way to the visitor center at the Cape Cod National Seashore. There are many places you can stop. Take a dip. Have a picnic. Hike or paddle to the seashore's marshes and lighthouses.

Make sure to treat yourself to some super-fresh seafood along the way. Visit one of the Cape's many clam or lobster shacks. These roadside restaurants are fun and delicious. Sink your spoon into a bowl of clam chowder. Snack on a tasty lobster roll.

Decide for yourself which Cape Cod lobster shack has the best lobster rolls.

CAPE ANN

Did you know that Massachusetts has not one but two capes? Cape Ann is on the North Shore of Massachusetts. Visit the fishing village of Gloucester and go for a whale watch. Or, take a short drive up to Rockport. Walk along the pier at Bearskin Neck. It got its name in the year 1700 when a bear got caught in the ocean tide.

TAKE A TRIP TO THE 1600s!

> Do you wish you could travel back nearly four hundred years? Step back in time to Plimoth Plantation. Learn what life was like for an English colonist in 1600s Massachusetts. Plymouth was the first permanent English colony in America. At Plimoth Plantation, you can visit colonists inside their homes. Share a meal with the pilgrims at the first Thanksgiving. Hear livestock braying and baaing. You can visit a Wampanoag village too. Talk with modern members of the Wampanoag tribe about life in the 1600s.

You could arrive at Plymouth on the *Mayflower* back in 1620. Come aboard the *Mayflower II*. This replica is the same size as the original *Mayflower* ship. It is 106 feet (32.3 meters) long, but it is only 25 feet (7.6 m) wide. Imagine how small the ship must have felt to the pilgrims!

THE WAMPANOAG

The English were not the first people to live in Massachusetts. The Wampanoag had called the area home for more than ten thousand years. At first, Wampanoag leader Massasoit made a peace treaty with the English. Years later, the English intruded on the Wampanoag's lands. The Wampanoag's new leader, Metacom, tried to drive the English out by force. The violence resulted in many deaths among the Wampanoag.

The *Mayflower II* is a replica of the ship that brought the Pilgrims to Massachusetts in 1620.

At Plimoth Plantation, actors role-play English colonists who help you experience colonial Plymouth.

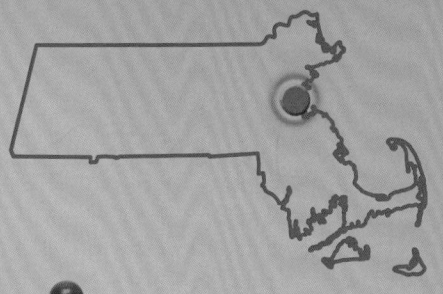

WELCOME TO THE PUBLIC GARDEN

Make Way for Ducklings, by Robert McCloskey, is Massachusetts's official state children's book.

> Come smell the roses in the United States' first public botanical garden. The city of Boston created the Public Garden in 1837. It was created for the city's citizens and visitors to enjoy.

Stroll the paths of the Public Garden. You will notice many monuments, statues, and fountains. Can you find the statue of Mrs. Mallard and her eight ducklings? They are characters from the famous children's book *Make Way for Ducklings*. There is even a lagoon. Here ducks and other waterbirds splash and paddle.

Swan boats also paddle in the lagoon. These paddleboats are powered by a captain on a bicycle. The boats' bicycles are hidden by swan sculptures. Riding a swan boat through the Public Garden is an experience you can't miss.

The Public Garden's bronze statue of George Washington on horseback is the largest sculpture in Boston.

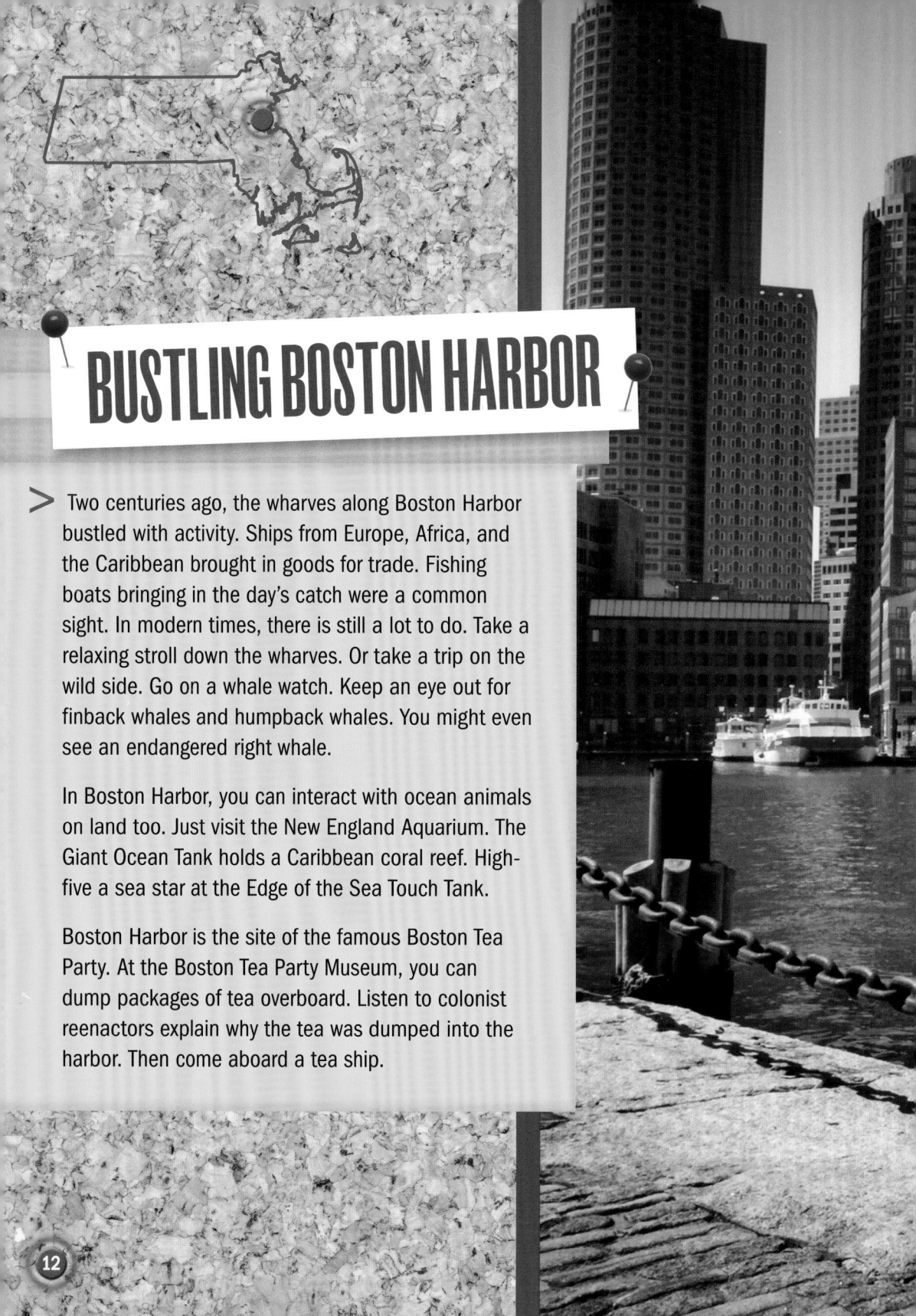

BUSTLING BOSTON HARBOR

> Two centuries ago, the wharves along Boston Harbor bustled with activity. Ships from Europe, Africa, and the Caribbean brought in goods for trade. Fishing boats bringing in the day's catch were a common sight. In modern times, there is still a lot to do. Take a relaxing stroll down the wharves. Or take a trip on the wild side. Go on a whale watch. Keep an eye out for finback whales and humpback whales. You might even see an endangered right whale.

In Boston Harbor, you can interact with ocean animals on land too. Just visit the New England Aquarium. The Giant Ocean Tank holds a Caribbean coral reef. High-five a sea star at the Edge of the Sea Touch Tank.

Boston Harbor is the site of the famous Boston Tea Party. At the Boston Tea Party Museum, you can dump packages of tea overboard. Listen to colonist reenactors explain why the tea was dumped into the harbor. Then come aboard a tea ship.

More than two thousand fish live in the Caribbean coral reef in the Giant Ocean Tank at the New England Aquarium.

BOSTON TEA PARTY

On December 16, 1773, US patriots, disguised as Mohawk American Indians, snuck aboard tea ships in Boston Harbor. They threw more than 340 chests of tea overboard. The patriots were protesting a British tax on tea that they thought was unfair. The tea they dumped was worth £18,000 (British pounds) at that time. That's about $3.6 million today. Now that's a lot of tea!

FOLLOW THE FREEDOM TRAIL!

> The Freedom Trail is a fun way to experience Massachusetts history. The 2.5-mile (4 km) trail takes you to sixteen places that were important during the Revolutionary War (1775–1783). Bricks or a painted red line mark the trail on Boston's sidewalks. Tourists and Bay Staters alike follow the Freedom Trail.

On the Freedom Trail, learn about Boston's role in the Revolutionary War. Take a peek inside Paul Revere's house. Or sit in a pew at the Old North Church. That's where lanterns were lit to alert patriots if the British were coming. Patriots were said to light one lantern if the British were coming by land and two if by sea.

The warship USS *Constitution* is another stop on the trail. It is also known as Old Ironsides. The ship earned its nickname in the War of 1812. A British ship fired cannonballs at it. The cannonballs bounced off the sides of the USS *Constitution*. It seemed as if the ship was made of iron, not wood.

BATTLE OF BUNKER HILL

One stop on the Freedom Trail is the Bunker Hill Monument. It marks the spot of the first major battle of the American Revolutionary War. The Americans lost the Battle of Bunker Hill. But the English lost a lot of soldiers. It was one of the first signs that the patriots would not give up. It helped boost support for the Revolution.

Every year, more than 3.2 million people walk Boston's Freedom Trail.

Along the Freedom Trail

Faneuil Hall

State St.

The Old State House

Site of the Boston Massacre

King's Chapel & Burying Ground

Court St.

Tremont St.

School St.

Washington St.

Old South Meeting House

N

Arch St.

Devonshire St.

Water St.

Milk St.

Congress St.

The USS *Constitution* is the oldest commissioned warship in the world.

15

BIRTHPLACE OF A NATION

> Boston was not the only site of revolutionary events in Massachusetts. You can walk in the footsteps of the minutemen in Concord and Lexington. Minutemen were volunteer soldiers in the American Revolutionary War. They had to be ready to fight at a minute's notice.

At Minute Man National Historical Park, explore the same fields minutemen did in 1775. Watch a movie called *The Road to Revolution* to learn more about Paul Revere's ride and the start of the Revolutionary War. Then, walk across the wooden planks of the North Bridge in Concord. That's where minutemen challenged British troops patrolling the bridge. Imagine how it felt to be a minuteman on the bridge.

On Patriots' Day—which falls on the third Monday of April—you can even watch the battle that started it all. Every year, people reenact the Battle of Lexington on the town green. It takes place at 5:45 a.m. That's the time the real battle took place in 1775. Afterward, don't miss the Patriots' Day Parade and pancake breakfast.

Reenactors play the part of soldiers in His Majesty's Tenth Regiment of Foot (the British Redcoats) or the Lexington Minute Men Company.

HENRY DAVID THOREAU

In the 1800s, Concord was home to writer Henry David Thoreau. When he was twenty-seven, Thoreau moved from town to a cabin he built on nearby Walden Pond. There, he wrote *Walden*. This is a book of essays about living in the woods. Thoreau was an important figure in American literature.

FALL FUN

> Fall is a special time in Massachusetts. In mid-September, leaves start changing color from green to orange, yellow, and red. This brings out a special kind of visitor called a leaf peeper. Massachusetts's fun fall activities might bring out the leaf peeper in you!

Want a bird's-eye view of the fall colors? Then take the sky ride up Wachusett Mountain in Princeton. Or for a view closer to sea level, take a scenic car trip to the Northern Berkshire Fall Foliage Festival Parade. It is held in October in North Adams. Be sure to go on the annual leaf hunt after the parade. Find the paper leaves hidden around the town to earn a prize.

Visit an apple orchard to pick your own apples. Many orchards have other fun activities such as mazes, hayrides, and even petting zoos. In the fall, Massachusetts's cranberry bogs are loaded with red berries ready to be picked. You can tour a cranberry farm to learn more about growing cranberries. Visit Wareham on the South Shore for the annual Cranberry Harvest Celebration.

Sip a cup of apple cider or chomp on a cider doughnut at one of Massachusetts's many apple orchards.

Southeastern Massachusetts and Cape Cod are home to more than 14,000 acres (5,665 hectares) of working cranberry bogs.

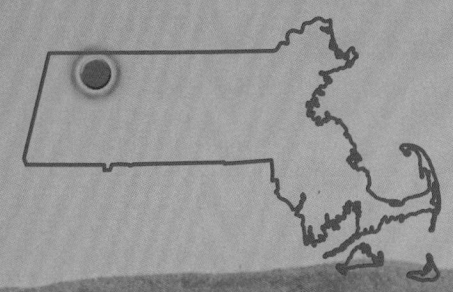

THE MOHAWK TRAIL

> One great way to see the beautiful Berkshire Hills is to follow the Mohawk Trail in Western Massachusetts. The trail is named after the Mohawk people native to the area. This scenic drive starts at the border of Massachusetts and New York. It winds along all the way to the Connecticut border. Marvel at the rock formations carved by glaciers thousands of years ago. See North America's only naturally formed marble arch bridge at Natural Bridge State Park.

After your car ride, step inside some of Western Massachusetts's many museums. Stop at the Eric Carle Museum of Picture Book Art. Eric Carle is the author and illustrator of the famous picture book *The Very Hungry Caterpillar.* At the museum, you can look at illustrations from your favorite picture books by other artists too. See art from *Madeleine*; *Lyle, Lyle Crocodile*; and *Don't Let the Pigeon Drive the Bus!*

Did you know Dr. Seuss was born in Western Massachusetts? The town of Springfield was his boyhood home. Now, it is the home of the Dr. Seuss National Memorial Sculpture Garden. Find statues of your favorite characters. Can you spot the Cat in the Hat, Horton the Elephant, and the Lorax?

See your favorite Dr. Seuss characters come to life at the Dr. Seuss Sculpture Garden in Springfield.

The White Marble Dam at Natural Bridge State Park was built in the early 1800s.

A COLLEGE FOR EVERY STUDENT

> Did you know that there are about 120 colleges in Massachusetts? More than 150,000 students go to Boston's many colleges and universities. With so many schools to choose from, maybe you'll find your perfect school in Massachusetts. Harvard University and the University of Massachusetts (UMass) Amherst are two that are fun to visit.

Harvard University in Cambridge is the most famous Boston-area school. It was established in 1636. That's only sixteen years after the pilgrims landed in Plymouth! Harvard is the oldest university in the United States. Stop by the Harvard Information Center to take a historical tour. Walk in the footsteps of famous Harvard graduates. President Barack Obama, Microsoft founder Bill Gates, and Facebook founder Mark Zuckerberg all went to school there.

In Western Massachusetts, visit the large campus of the UMass Amherst. Students there can study to be a teacher, an engineer, a nurse, or even a musician! The university is tucked into the town of Amherst. Stroll through downtown or take the trolley. Visit the Toy Box toy shop or lick an ice-cream cone at Bart's Amherst Ice Cream.

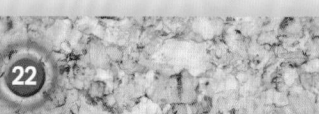

Tour Boston Harbor with UMass Amherst mascot Sam the Minuteman before a football game at Gillette Stadium.

Visit the famous statue of John Harvard by Daniel Chester French in the Old Yard section of Harvard Yard.

FENWAY PARK

> At more than one hundred years old, Fenway Park is one of the United States' most famous baseball parks. The Boston Red Sox call the park baseball's House of Worship. Many other baseball players agree. Former baseball player Cal Ripken Jr. once said of Fenway, "The thing that I remember the most is just the feeling you get when you walk out on that field....It's just a great feeling to be able to play baseball on that field. It's a special place."

Why is Fenway Park so special? The oldest park in Major League Baseball (MLB) keeps a lot of its original charm. It is the smallest Major League Baseball park in the country. Fans sit on seats made of solid oak rather than plastic.

The famous Green Monster that overlooks left field is a major landmark. The 37-foot (11.2 m) wall is home to Fenway Park's scoreboard. It is one of the last hand-operated boards in the country. Two employees who work inside the wall change the numbers. They also flash green and red lights to signal balls and strikes. Take a tour of Fenway Park when you visit Massachusetts. It's one of the state's top ten!

Fenway Park would not be Fenway Park without the 37-foot-tall (11.2 m) Green Monster wall that overlooks the stadium (*above*). You might even get to meet Wally the Green Monster, the Red Sox mascot (*left*).

YOUR TOP TEN!

You've read about ten awesome things to see and do in Massachusetts. Now it's time to think about what *your* Massachusetts top ten list would include. What would you like to see if you visited the state? What would you be most excited about if you were planning a Massachusetts vacation? Write your list down on a separate sheet of paper. Turn your list into a book. Illustrate it with drawings or with pictures from the Internet or magazines.

MASSACHUSETTS BY MAP

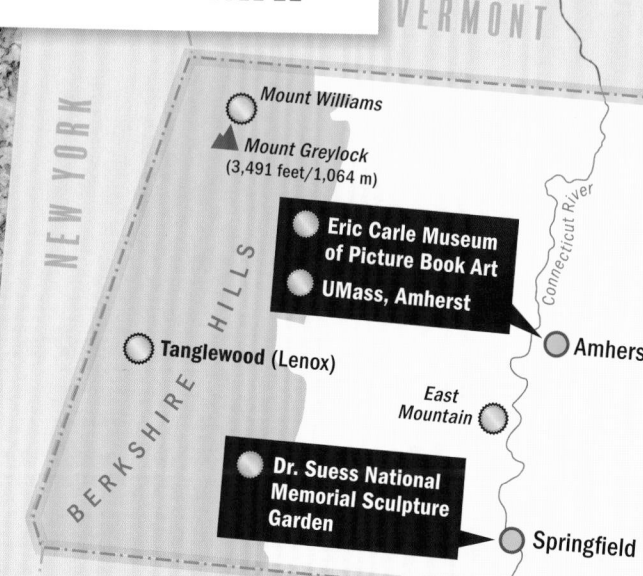

VERMONT

NEW YORK

Mount Williams

▲ Mount Greylock
(3,491 feet/1,064 m)

Connecticut River

Eric Carle Museum of Picture Book Art

UMass, Amherst

BERKSHIRE HILLS

Tanglewood (Lenox)

Amherst

East Mountain

Dr. Suess National Memorial Sculpture Garden

Springfield

CONNECTICUT

N

> MAP KEY

⊛ Capital city

○ City

◎ Point of interest

▲ Highest elevation

–·– State border

Visit www.lerneresource.com to learn more about the state flag of Massachusetts.

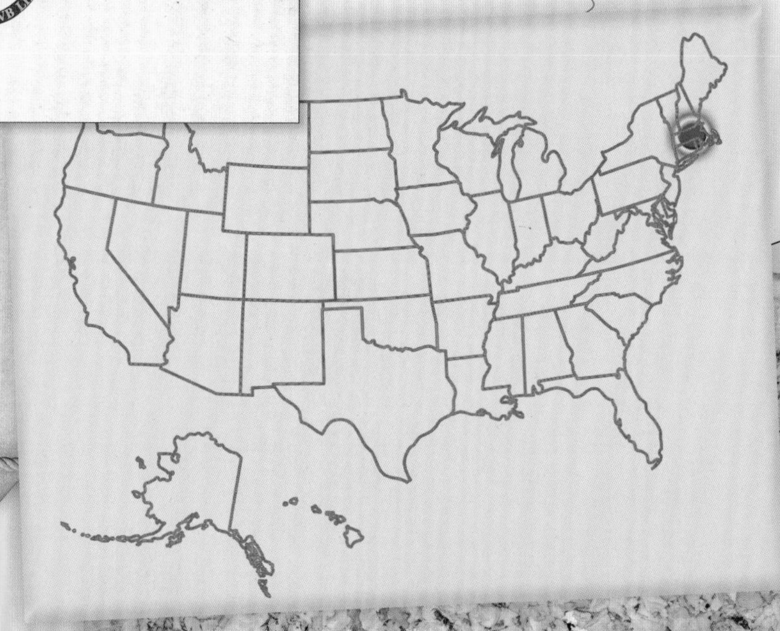

ENSE PETIT PLACIDAM SVB LIBERTATE

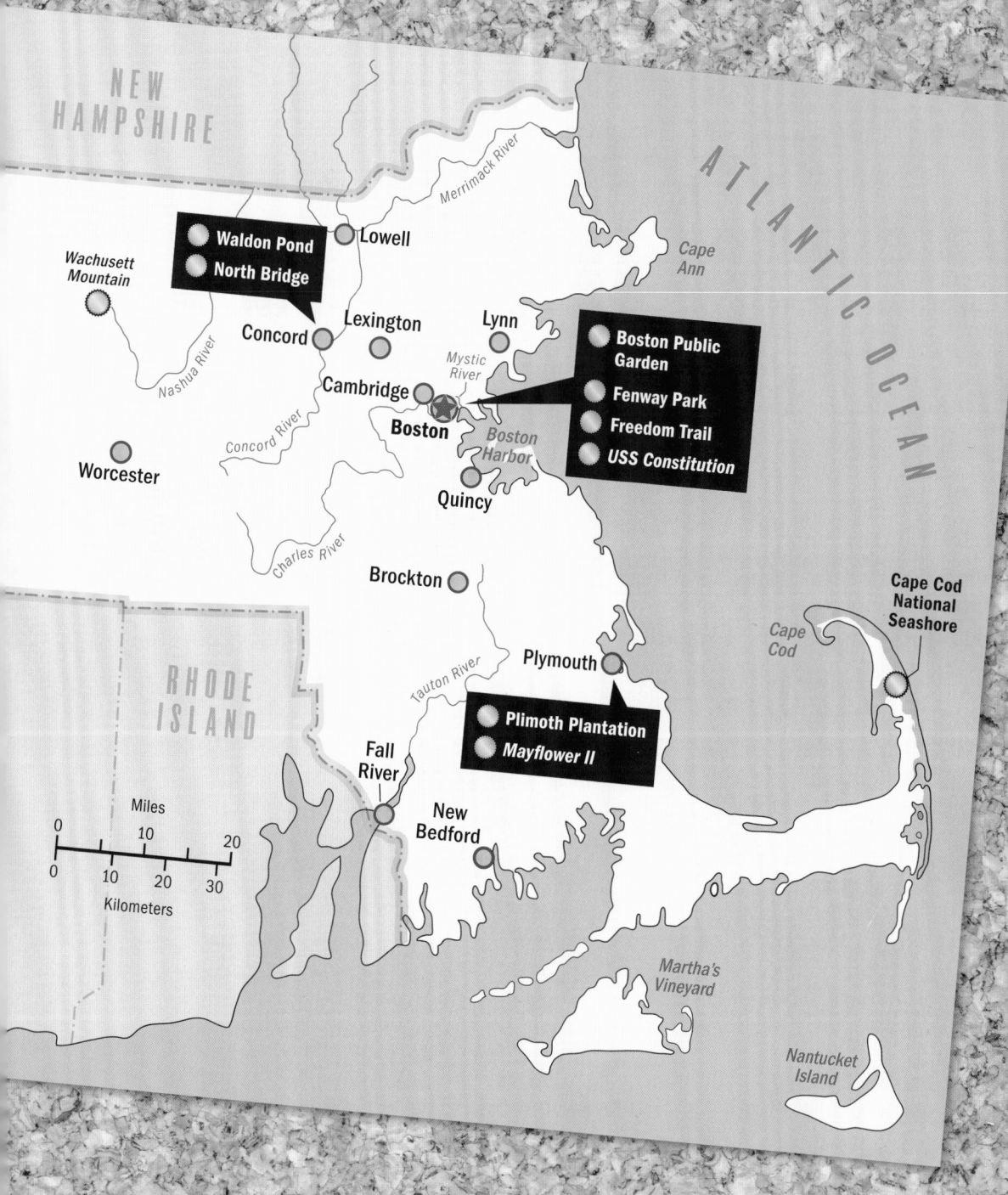

NEW HAMPSHIRE

ATLANTIC OCEAN

Merrimack River

Cape Ann

Wachusett Mountain

Waldon Pond
North Bridge

Lowell

Lexington

Lynn

Boston Public Garden
Fenway Park
Freedom Trail
USS Constitution

Concord

Mystic River

Nashua River

Cambridge

Boston

Boston Harbor

Concord River

Worcester

Quincy

Charles River

Brockton

Cape Cod National Seashore

Tauton River

Plymouth

Cape Cod

RHODE ISLAND

Plimoth Plantation
Mayflower II

Fall River

New Bedford

Miles
0   10   20
0   10   20   30
Kilometers

Martha's Vineyard

Nantucket Island

MASSACHUSETTS FACTS

NICKNAMES: Bay State, Old Bay State, Old Colony State, Puritan State, Baked Bean State

SONGS: "All Hail to Massachusetts" by Arthur Marsh, "Massachusetts" by Arlo Guthrie (adopted July 1981)

MOTTO: *Ense petit placidam sub libertate quietem*, or "By the sword we seek peace, but peace only under liberty"

> **FLOWER:** mayflower

TREE: American elm

> **BIRD:** black-capped chickadee

ANIMALS: Boston terrier, right whale

> **FOODS:** corn muffin, cranberry juice, Boston cream pie, chocolate chip cookie

DATE AND RANK OF STATEHOOD: February 6, 1788; the 6th state

> **CAPITAL:** Boston

AREA: 8,257 square miles (21,398 sq. km)

AVERAGE JANUARY TEMPERATURE: 28.2°F (–2.1°C)

AVERAGE JULY TEMPERATURE: 72.0°F (22.2°C)

POPULATION AND RANK: 6,646,144; 14th (2012)

MAJOR CITIES AND POPULATIONS: Boston (626,479), Worcester (182,669), Springfield (153,552), Lowell (108,552), Cambridge (106,471)

NUMBER OF US CONGRESS MEMBERS: 9 representatives, 2 senators

NUMBER OF ELECTORAL VOTES: 11

NATURAL RESOURCES: clay, lime, sand, gravel, silica, quartz, marble

AGRICULTURAL PRODUCTS: greenhouse/nursery plants, fruits and vegetables, cranberries, milk, livestock/poultry

MANUFACTURED GOODS: defense technology, information technology, biotechnology, films

STATE HOLIDAYS: Patriots' Day, Independence Day, Columbus Day

GLOSSARY

Bay Stater: the official name for someone who lives in Massachusetts

botanical: relating to plants

colonist: someone who lives in a colony, or area that is controlled by a country that is not near it

endangered: in danger of dying out

intruded: came to a place without being invited or welcome

minutemen: volunteer soldiers in the American Revolutionary War who were ready to fight at a minute's notice

North Shore: the part of Massachusetts north of Boston, including Gloucester and Cape Ann

reenactor: someone who acts out or performs again the actions of an earlier event

replica: an exact copy of something

South Shore: the part of Massachusetts south and east of Boston, including Plymouth and Cape Cod

wharf: a flat structure built along the shore used to dock ships and move cargo

LERNER

SOURCE

Expand learning beyond the printed book. Download free, complementary educational resources for this book from our website, www.lerneresource.com.

FURTHER INFORMATION

Gondosch, Linda. *How Did Tea and Taxes Spark a Revolution? And Other Questions about the Boston Tea Party*. Minneapolis: Lerner Publications, 2011. Learn more about why the Boston patriots tossed tea into the Boston Harbor In 1773.

Jerome, Kate Boehm. *Boston and the State of Massachusetts: Cool Stuff Every Kid Should Know*. Charleston, SC: Arcadia, 2011. Learn more fun facts about Massachusetts and its capital.

McCloskey, Robert. *Make Way for Ducklings*. New York: Viking Press, 1941. Meet the Mallard family in Massachusetts's official state children's book.

The Paul Revere House: Just for Kids
http://www.paulreverehouse.org/kids
Step into Paul Revere's house on a virtual visit! Learn more about the Boston patriot and his role in the American Revolutionary War.

Philbrick, Nathaniel. *The Mayflower and the Pilgrims' New World*. New York: GP Putnam's Sons, 2008. Discover what it was like to travel across the Atlantic Ocean on the *Mayflower*.

Plimoth Plantation: Investigating the First Thanksgiving
http://www.plimoth.org/media/olc/intro.html
With the help of Sarah and Dancing Hawk, learn more about the first Thanksgiving and why historians think a better name is "1621 Harvest Celebration."

Secretary of the Commonwealth's Kids' Zone
http://www.sec.state.ma.us/cis/ciskid/kididx.htm
Are you a history buff? Check out the Kids' Zone to play Massachusetts state trivia and solve a Bay State word scramble.

INDEX

PHOTO ACKNOWLEDGMENTS

The images in this book are used with the permission of: © Axiom Photographic/Design Pics/Corbis, p. 1; © Robert Landau/Corbis, pp. 4–5, 18–19; © spirit of america/Shutterstock Images, pp. 4, 20–21; © Laura Westlund/Independent Picture Service, pp. 5, 26–27, 26 (bottom); © Jim West/imagebroker/Corbis, pp. 6–7; © Olga Lyubkina/Shutterstock Images, p. 7 (top); © dp Photography/Shutterstock Images, p. 7 (bottom); © Andreas Juergensmeier/Shutterstock Images, pp. 8–9; © Kevin Fleming/Corbis, pp. 9 (top), 13 (top); © Robert Holmes/Corbis, p. 9 (bottom); © Amanda Hall/Robert Harding World Imagery/Corbis, pp. 10–11; © aceshot1/Shutterstock Images, p. 10; © Jorge Salcedo/Shutterstock Images, pp. 11, 14–15, 23 (bottom); © boblin/iStockphoto, pp. 12–13; © Marcos Carvalho/Shutterstock Images, p. 13 (bottom); © Ryan Angelo/Shutterstock Images, p. 14; © Laughing Stock/Corbis, p. 15 (top); © BKingFoto/Shutterstock Images, p. 15 (bottom); © jmorse2000/iStockphoto, pp. 16–17; © Kelly-Mooney Photography/Corbis, p. 17 (top); © wynnter/iStockphoto, p. 17 (bottom); © Lori Sparkia/Shutterstock Images, p. 19 (top); © Xuanlu Wang/Shutterstock Images, p. 19 (bottom); © DayTripsAtHand.com, p. 21 (top); © Stuwrtlttle/Dreamstime.com, p. 21 (bottom); © Topic Photo Agency/Corbis, pp. 22–23; © KenWiedemann/iStockphoto p. 23 (top); © Brian Jenkins/Corbis, pp. 24–25; © Michael Tureski/Icon SMI, p. 25 (left); © Eugene Buchko/Shutterstock Images, p. 25 (right); © nicoolay/iStockphoto, 26 (top); © Roger Whiteway/iStockphoto, p. 29 (top); © Mr_Jamsey/iStockphoto, p. 29 (middle top); © maxfeld/Shutterstock Images, p. 29 (middle bottom); © Deejpilot/iStockphoto, p. 29 (bottom).

Cover: © Shutterstock.com (beach), © istockphoto.com/Songquan Deng (Fenway Park); © iStockphoto.com/drnadig (USS Constitution); © Laura Westlund/Independent Picture Service (map); © iStockphoto.com/fpm (seal); © iStockphoto.com/vicm (pushpins); © iStockphoto.com/benz190 (cork board).